For Those Who Wander

For anyone who has wanted someone to believe
in them

Let Me Write

Let me write

And say these words with ease

The suffocating judgments

Will come, and they'll squeeze

Give me Bryon, and Chopin

Inspiration at its best

Give me Hemingway, and Woolf

In peace may they rest

Let me write

These thoughts weigh a ton

To create is my addiction

And I've only just begun

Give Until They Bleed

The fog-filled her head

As the work continued to pour

She thought a change would come

This time, something more

You can always tell who they are

The fighters behind the scenes

They give and give and give

They give until they bleed

Whispers

Can you hear them yelling?

They are screaming from their lungs

They want to be free

In their blood they are still young

Dreaming of the days

When their voices would be heard

You can hear them in the woods

When their whispers have been stirred

All it Needs to Hear is You

Let the Universe take the lead

Be happy be free

Don't let the day weigh you down

Never carry with you a frown

It won't be like this forever

Mind and body go together

Tell yourself nice things

Believe it to be true

The Universe is listening

All it needs to hear is you

How Long Will We Wait

What can I say

These thoughts linger

Leaving quite a taste

I'm not a fan of bitter

Take a sip of Guinness

The words come with ease

They taste even better

But float away with the breeze

If they don't hear

I'll write until it bleeds

My heart I will follow

Adventure it desperately needs

You can wonder forever

But where will that go

Bring it to life

Time doesn't wait for the flow

They will pass by

Years not yet lived

How long will we wait

To our dreams, we will give

Never Go Without

Wild as the wolves

She was bound and determined

Fearless in the pursuit

Her hunt was not the burden

Never go without

Your optimism and your peace

Others will try and capture

But her truth the earth would keep

Follow Your Intuition

The wind tells a story

Only I can hear at times

In the wild, I'm at peace

As the trees listen to my rhymes

This path might dead end

Or take another turn

Follow your intuition

It's there for you to learn

Grief Can Weigh A Ton

They said that it would hurt

In time I'd start to heal

Maybe it wouldn't hurt so much

If only I didn't feel

But nothing they said was true

My heart breaks more and more each day

I try to drown out that memory

It hurts is all I can say

Moments are harder than others

Grief can weigh a ton

He wasn't just my dog

To me, he was my son

Take A Closer Look

There is magic in the madness

Take a closer look

Write a brand new chapter

Re-read your favorite book

Take a chance and create

Your world from a different view

Possibility is everywhere

All it's waiting for is you

Let it All Breathe

It took some time

But she soon realized

She didn't have to hold so tight

To the worries, she had fantasized

Let it all breathe

Time will achieve

What's meant for her

She will receive

She's Lost Can't You See

In a search to find

Just where she lost her mind

It was just here

Choices made seemed so clear

Now there's just a blur

Does anyone know a cure

She's lost can't you see

Burdens and sadness buried her deep

Screams from her soul began

Please make me whole once again

I Want Fire

I want passion

I want fire

Living breathing dreams

That takes me higher

I want wild

I want peace

Feeding my soul

With adventures, I seek

Feel Every Single Part

How will you know

Which path is meant for you

Is there one in particular

Or maybe quite a few

Do you ride through the night

Keeping secrets to yourself

Or do you run through the wild

Screaming for some help

Trust your intuition

Feel every single part

Live in the present

You'll never know unless you start

My Dear, You Are Alive

Silly little fears

That sing inside your head

They run around like monsters

And hide under your bed

You tried not to feed them

Realizing this could make it worse

As you look inside the mirror

And ask if you've been cursed

My dear, you are alive

Bless your heart you didn't know

It's when you learn your fears

That dreams begin to grow

Ready To Take It On

I can't breathe

I think it's time to leave

Their demands are never-ending

Frankly, I'm tired of bending

I crave life and something whole

What happened to their souls

How can you feed creativity

When this place only runs on negativity

Ready to take it on

Before they know it I will be gone

Whatever Your Reasons Are

How do you see yourself

Are you living or existing

If someone were to ask you

Would you say it's passion you're persisting

Are you afraid of change

Or fear of uncertainty

Whatever your reasons are

I hope you choose to live fearlessly

Be Honest With Yourself

What inspires you

Is it passion and fire

Are you staying true

Does it fuel your desires

Are you afraid of failures

Be honest with yourself

If you don't take the risks

How will you know how it felt

To accomplish makes you feel alive

The good you feel like a natural high

Remind them who's trapped inside

The need to hide no longer abides

Your Dreams Don't Need a Key

Tell me something dear

How many times have you been here

Did you get lost on your way

You asked your heart

What did it say

I asked mine once before to

Thinking I'd get a clue

It said I've been here all along

Singing you this song

Trust in me you'll see

Your dreams don't need a key

You have the power to create

Your passions are your fate

Gentle Moon

Gentle moon

Kiss me with your light

I'm grateful for your energy

Falling in love with the night

Together They Share So Beautifully

I love the night

And how it greets the sun

Welcoming its rays

As the daylight says I'm done

Together they share so beautifully

Taking turns for their love

We could learn from them

Give equally and rise above

Never Lose Sight

I lit the path

So, I could see

The stars helped too

Illuminating the way for me

I may go left

I may go right

Whichever way I choose

I will never lose sight

For All to See

Share your light

For all to see

Don't hide in the shadows

To be yourself

Is a deep-rooted need

A Place For Thoughts To Go

I read their words

I'm blown away

Do you think they knew

Their thoughts forever to stay

I am in awe of their minds

And the places they take me to

Inspiring new writers

Like me and like you

Writing heals the soul

A place for thoughts to go

Creating inspiration

A place for us to grow

Thank You For Your Patience

Dear future self

Thank you for your courage

If it wasn't for your risks

I'd feel defeated and discouraged

Thank you for never letting me

Forget how far I've come

That child deep inside of me

Who felt the urge to run

Thank you for your patience

Your devotion to pursue

I appreciate all you taught me

Thank you for being you

Stay Wild in Your Path

The moon told me tonight

To be honest with myself

Am I prepared for what's to come

Practice gratitude above all else

Patience is a lesson

We must often learn to gain

Stay wild in your path

But allow honesty to remain

Ink Upon the Page

There is a light inside

Dying to get out

Hiding behind the eyes

From the soul, it wants to shout

Fingertips that spill

Ink upon the page

Enchanted by the power

History to be made

In Forms of Poetry

There is magic in her bones

Aching to be free

Spells flowing from her lips

In forms of poetry

A Life Without Imagination

Mysterious thoughts

Fed her curiosity

A life without imagination

An absurd monstrosity

Fearless At Its Best

Foolish to believe

You are comparable to the rest

You are valiant my dear

Fearless at its best

Green Eyes Tell a Story

Enchanted by the moon

Allured by its glow

Green eyes tell a story

That only she could know

Take a glance if you must

Deep into her stare

Get lost inside the charm

Her magic if you dare

Without Any Conditions

Powerful women

Led by men

Have we not learned anything

From where we've been

Why are our minds

Still up for the proposition

We deserve to make our choices

Without any conditions

The Shedding of The Old

Oh, how they change

The colors of the season

Without explanation

Nor rhyme or reason

The shedding of the old

Brings days of new

Before your very eyes

The Earth says thank you

They Lie Within us All

I enjoy looking up

As opposed to

Looking down

Many say I'm optimistic

It's better than a frown

I find it soothes my soul

To see possibilities

They lie within us all

Imagine your abilities

Lift Each Other Up

Should I have

To share my story

To gain your respect

I am the definition

Of persistence

Your ignorance I reject

Lift each other up

Stop looking so appalled

I didn't get here

Taking it easy

I walked before

I crawled

From My Soul To Yours

As I take a deep breathe

Inhaling peace

From my soul to yours

Exhale and release

I Nourished My Roots

I raised my height

So you could see me

I grew more leaves

The birds carefree

I strengthened my limbs

For others to climb

I nourished my roots

Evolution takes time

I Am Your Voice

I am the words

That fill the page

I am the thoughts

Brought to life

I am the ink

On your fingers

I am your voice

That cuts like a knife

I write

It's what I do

I write

For people like you

Now More Than Ever

Here we are

In a world

Full of change

Some are

Spewing hate

Some are

Feeling strange

This is the time

Now more

Then ever

To put aside

Our differences

Support

And come together

Let Them Roam

Who are you

To decide their fate

A trophy for your mantle

A wall to decorate

Give them peace

Let them roam

The Earth was theirs

Long before it was

Our home

Silent Pleas

I know it's not just me

Within their eyes

Are silent pleas

We are living

In a haze

Holding out

For better days

Under Majestic Skies

Winter days

Spent by the fire

Spring's sun rays

Lift spirits higher

Summer nights

Full of fireflies

Colors of fall

Under majestic skies

Nostalgia

Nostalgia
A sentimental longing
For somewhere I know
A feeling of belonging
Perhaps it'll come to me
Awakened from a dream
Then slide through
My fingertips
Revealing an empty scene
It's there
Deep inside my bones
This thing I know so well
All I have is time
And a thousand
Stories to tell

Live in The Moment

Love is timeless

Music too

Live in the moment

The day is new

Felt Deep Inside

A poet writes the lyrics

For words left unsaid

Felt deep inside

Your bones

The thoughts

In your head

The pen is my mic

As I sing out

These dreams

Poetry and music

Meeting at the seams

It Takes Time

Please don't take offense

If my actions don't make sense

Creatives need their space

It takes time to cultivate

Make A Wish

Close your eyes

Make a wish

The dark and light

Both exist

A whisper

From your soul

A spell to be told

It's Here Where I can Learn

I find comfort

In the solitude

It's here where

I can learn

What it is

That drives me

Like a book

My pages turn

The Day is New

Take a deep breath
The day is new
Tomorrow isn't here
Let the present
Soak into you

I Am Giddy

I always look

Forward to tomorrow

And what it will bring

Like a child

I am giddy

A bird with

Brand new wings

Dare To Be

Who you are today

Changed since yesterday

Allow yourself to grow

The courage to say no

Dare to be

Exceptional in

Your weirdness

Find comfort

In your skin

The courage to

Be fearless

Hidden By Disguises

Monsters come in

All shapes and sizes

Looking quite innocent

Hidden by disguises

Stay conscious

Of the dark

But remain

In the light

The sun feeds

Your soul

As well as

The night

As The Years Pass

I have a wildness

Inside me

That can't be tamed

As the years' pass

The more of me

It claims

Feed Into Your Soul

At some point today

Give yourself a smile

You don't know how

Incredibly strong you are

You've walked an

Unbearable mile

Plant the seeds

For tomorrow

Feed into your soul

Give yourself some love

Let go of what

You can't control

In The Darkness

She's reminded

In the darkness

Of the strength

That lies within

How incredible it is

Each day

A chance to begin

Helped Me Grow

Past loves

Memories of

Who I'm not

Can't be caught

Thank you though

Helped me grow

A gypsy soul

Feeling whole

Wild From Within

I feel it all

Deep inside

Even the dark

Has a place to hide

Painted flesh

My body

My canvas

Wild from within

I came from

Atlantis

I Live To Dream

I read my books

I believe in wonder

I love the blues

I enjoy the thunder

I will never settle

I live to dream

I say what I think

I lay in moonbeams

You Already Knew

I asked the stars
To give me a clue
They said, my dear
You already knew
Powerful intuition
With a gift of sight
You have all you need
On this night

Make it Count

Rise and shine

This day is mine

Make it count

Remove all doubt

We have 24 hours

They should

Be devoured

Gives Me Peace

Are you lonely

Asked the moon

Not anymore,

Said the woman

Your glow

It gives me peace

More than any

Other human

This Place is Mine Alone

I like where I am at

It fits just like a hat

I wasn't sure before

Now I want it even more

This place is mine alone

I think it feels like home

My how I have grown

As I venture into

The unknown

Feel Every Single Moment

Be gentle

With yourself

You're doing

All you can

Feel every

Single moment

know when to

Take a stand

How I Got This Way

Ask me what

Inspires me

I'll sing of

Books and music

Ask me how

I got this way

My words

May be elusive

I feel The Need

When the moon is full
I feel the need
To quench a thirst
Something to feed

Every Little Drop

I look at everything

The beauty and the gore

Life is exhilarating

Leaves me wanting more

My passions run deep

Coursing through my veins

I use every little drop

Creativity without the chains

The Person Inside

I was in a cage

And didn't know

The person inside

Needed to grow

Unaware of the limits

I set for myself

Like a book

I've been opened

No longer

On the shelf

Matches My Own

I asked the moon

To lie with me

Rest deep inside

My bones

I've been here along

She said

Your soul

Matches my own

Minutes Later

Late last night

I thought I

Heard the

Howling

It was only

Minutes later

Against my skin

I felt

The growling

Burning Bright

I hold a fire

Within me

Burning bright

Beneath my skin

Past lives

Coming forth

Ready to begin

No Need To Hide

Hold tight to that

Feeling inside

The one that

Reminds you

There is no

Need to hide

Your existence

Is beautiful

In all of its glory

You are meant

To do so much

Let today

Be a part

Of your story

Be Careful Not To Feed It

Smile everyday

Keep up with the notion

Revealing nothing at all

This is your daily potion

What kind of life is that

A wolf can never be caged

Deceit presents itself

As actors on a stage

Resentment is quite ugly

As it grows like a weed

Be careful not to feed it

Remain truthful

And take heed

The Universe Knew

Not by chance

Something more

The Universe knew

To open this door

From The Stars

Neither one

Looking

For the other

From the stars

A love

To discover

How Beautiful

Oh, how beautiful it is

When you

Sync into me

Together We Move

We danced

Under the moon

Bodies swaying

To nature's tune

Lost in the rhythms

Heartbeats

And wild sounds

Together we move

Love we have found

Nestled in Your Soul

Completely open

Naked and exposed

To the warmth

You have created

Nestled in your soul

A breath of fresh air

As it flows

Across my skin

Recognition from the past

A knowing

From within

Breathe Strength

Shed light on

The darkness

Breathe strength

Into my lungs

Words of admiration

Flowing from

My tongue

Slay in Their Armor

Hero's, we call them

As they slay

In their armor

Their battles go unseen

Every day getting stronger

You mustn't underestimate

Or laugh and

Cast your stones

The one you least expected

Will send shivers

Through your soul

Feel It

If it hurts

Let it

If you're angry

Feel it

Allow it to touch

The parts of you

Hiding beneath

The surface

Then let it go

And whisper

This no longer

Serves a purpose

We're Alive

Can we look

At the stars

And remember

We're alive

The days they

Go so quickly

You and I

Are meant to thrive

Remembering

Courage

The voice

That screams

Within

A reminder

To be brave

Remembering

Where you've been

In Your Arms

I never thought

I'd say

In your arms

Is where I'll stay

My heart has

Found its home

The Wandering Soul

No longer roams

Not One Can Convey

I try to come up

With better words to say

To describe what I feel

Not one can convey

Every time I try

Somehow you knew

Whispering the words

I love you

Head Held High

Respect should not

Come in waves

Leaving you

Running back

To your cage

Stand your ground

Head held high

You deserve

It all

Let your

Light shine

I'll Always Know

I was hoping

It'd be different

This time that

You would choose me

But I see

You haven't changed

You can have

Your high society

I'll always know

The truth about you

And who you

Could never be

I always hoped

For something more

In the end

I choose me

You Remind Me

In all my life

I've never felt

So safe

You make me

Come alive

You remind me

I am brave

One Look

One look

That was all it took

Your eyes are

My favorite book

Beware of The Wolf

I've got a story to tell

That is sure to entice

Other versions before

Were not so precise

Beware of the wolf

Disguised in

Sheep's clothing

They can't

Hide forever

When the

Truths approaching

The Reason

You're the reason

To my morning

The reason

For my smile

You're the one

That inspires me

To go that extra mile

A Love Like Ours

I knew who to look for

I'd recognize his heart

I looked into his eyes

And knew we'd never part

Loyal and loving

Protective in nature

A love like ours

There is nothing greater

Without Doubt

Without doubt

Or hesitation

I am

Undeniably yours

Loving your heart

As my own

As I will

Forevermore

I Think I Can Reach

How far can I see

She asked the tree

How high can you climb

I've been here a long time

I think I can reach

Could you help

Could you teach

In The Moons Light

In awe of its beauty

So she takes a closer look

The creatures in the dark

Were the same as in her books

In the moon's light

Shadows begin to appear

A haunted feeling

In the air

For her

A delightful cheer

Flaws and All

A sprinkle here

A sprinkle there

A dash of courage

I shall wear

I've made it this far

Flaws and all

I'll pick myself up

Each time I fall

Carry Me Across The Sea

Oh raven, sweet raven

Carry me across the sea

For I have found my one true love

And he is waiting for me

Oh raven, sweet raven

I ask this of thee

Fly me with your wings of might

So, my love, I shall see

Far Between

A safe place to land

At the end of my day

For you a quiet to the storms

You encounter on the way

I cherish these moments

At times they are few

And far between

The ones that only we see

Loving and serene

Magical Glow

Power within

Earth below

Moon ignites

A magical glow

Star Bright

Starlight

Star bright

This star

I see tonight

I shall wish

Upon you

With all

My might

You Cannot Corner

You cannot corner

What's not meant

To be tamed

For they will fight

Their fury inflamed

I Am Not Afraid

I am not afraid of who I am

Or what I have to say

I will hold my head up high

My thoughts will not be kept at bay

I have come too far for you

To validate my existence

Words mean nothing to me now

Action means persistence

I Listen

I listen for

The moon to say

Breathe my dear

It'll go the

Right way

A Conscious Decision

I've come to the conclusion

That only a few

Ever really listen

To hear another

You have to make

a conscious decision

Perhaps I think too much

My brain a constant flow

This is just an observation

From what I see

Come and go

Keep Safe

I want so badly

To protect you

From the monsters

In the dark

To take away

All of your fears

And keep safe

Your precious heart

I Hope

I never know

What I'll write

But I hope

That it might

Encourage you

To see

A world

Of possibilities

The Way I'm Made

I've always wondered

What it would be like

To be like the rest

A particular type

But then I realized

I do just fine

The way I'm made

A lovely design

Monsters Intuition

I often ask myself

Who I want to be

Not based on how

They see it

But who I am to me

This world can

Be ruthless

Inciting the

Monsters intuition

But I'd rather

Be the light

And stand with

The courage

Of my convictions

Live on Forever

Poets and painters

Singers and musicians

We're all sharing our souls

Growing from our creations

A word that links us all

A gift that can't be missed

One that will live on forever

My dear, that word is artist

Speak to Me

I miss being here

Surrounded by the trees

The woods speak to me

This is where

I find peace

Meet Me Tomorrow

I asked the night

To meet

Me tomorrow

Where my dreams

Will go

And intuition

To follow

I May Stay

I went into the woods

I may stay in here

Forever

A comfort

To my soul

It's beauty

Cannot

Be measured

Not to Settle

I welcome good energy

Removing the bad

You owe it

To yourself

Not to settle

For what you had

Appreciate the Dark

Each phase of the moon

Creates a new light

Some see darkness

While others ignite

Appreciate the dark

And what it has

To teach

For the moon

Is listening

Waiting to

Hear you speak

Rooted From the Ground

What moves you

Does it come

From deep within

Rooted from the ground

Etched beneath your skin

Driven to grow

In a direction

All your own

The will to stand tall

To use your backbone

Keep Talking

Why do the good

Always fight

The hardest

Against those

Who can't see

Past their own

Darkness

Keep going

Honest one

Your day will

Happen soon

But in the meantime

Keep talking

To the moon

Will Align

Just a pinch

Of encouragement

And a dash

Of ambition

The stars

Will align

And your dreams

To fruition

By Chance

Maybe tomorrow

Intentions to follow

It'll happen by chance

An urge to dance

Dare to dream

What this worlds

Never seen

It's not superstition

To trust your intuition

My Piece

Look at us all

Using our voices

The courage to stand

Make our own choices

I used to feel bad

For speaking my piece

I've come too far

The fear has ceased

Wandering Thoughts

A wandering soul

With wandering thoughts

In a web of dreams

My soul has

Been caught

Your Rules

I used to bite my tongue

Watching what I say

Hypocrisies

And judgments

The games people play

No longer will I sit idle

To your rules

I am a woman

Of courage

Not a little fool

A Kiss

I think to myself

As you lean in

For a kiss

All I've ever wanted

Is exactly this

Ambition Like Fire

If I just reach

A little bit higher

I could touch

The moon

With ambition

Like fire

Dancing across the sky

Tippy toes

And all

Reminds me

Of my courage

And my

Unwillingness

To fall

Our Time Has Come

Curious and mysterious

Excited and delirious

A hunt for the ages

Free from our cages

Our time has come

The bells have rung

No longer do we cower

This is the

Witching Hour

A Wanderer

Dear weeping willow

Can I rest here

On your bones

For I am but

A wanderer

Writing as

I roam

Evil Faces

Tis', not the night

That brings us fear

But the evil faces

Of the domineer

Calling Me

Waiting for the

Night to come

I hear the

Howling

And the drum

Calling me

Into the dark

A wild wolf

Must leave

Her mark

Made in the USA
Monee, IL
05 February 2023

27179317R00076